# FROM EGG TO CHICKEN

## Anita Ganeri

Heinemann Library
Chicago, Illinois

Designed by Ron Kamen and edesign
Printed and bound in China by South China Printing Company

10 09 08 07 06
10 9 8 7 6 5 4 3 2 1

**Library of Congress Cataloging-in-Publication Data**
Ganeri, Anita, 1961-
  From egg to chicken / Anita Ganeri.
    p. cm. -- (How living things grow)
  Includes bibliographical references.
  ISBN 1-4034-7858-9 (library binding - hardcover) -- ISBN 1-4034-7867-8 (pbk.)
  1. Chickens--Development--Juvenile literature. 2. Eggs--Juvenile literature. I. Title. II. Series.
  SF487.5G36 2006
  636.5'07--dc22

                              2005026922

**Acknowledgments**
The author and publishers are grateful to the following for permission to reproduce copyright material: Agripicture Images p. 5 (Peter Dean); Alamy pp. 6 (Tom Gundelwein), 14 (Chris Warham); 16 (Juncal); Animals Animals p. 17 (Jerry Cooke, Inc.); Ardea p. 10; Corbis p. 12 (Martin B. Withers/Frank Lane Picture Agency); FLPA p. 27 (SDK Maslowski); Geoff Hansen p. 13; Harcourt Education/Malcolm Harris pp. 11, 15, 20, 21, 22, 23, 24, 26; Getty Images p. 18 (photodisc); Holt Studios p. 7; Photolibrary.com pp. 8, 9; Science Photo Library p. 25 (Kenneth H. Thomas); Superstock pp. 4 (Pixtal), 19 (Jerry Downs).

Cover photograph of a chicken and egg reproduced with permission of Corbis/Brand X Pictures.

Illustrations by Martin Sanders.

Every effort has been made to contact copyright holders of any material reproduced in this book. Any omissions will be rectified in subsequent printings if notice is given to the publisher.

The paper used to print this book comes from sustainable resources.

# Some words are shown in bold, **like this**. You can find out what they mean by looking in the glossary.

# Contents

# Have You Ever Seen a Chicken?

A chicken is a kind of bird. It has feathers, wings, and a **beak**. People keep some chickens on farms. Eggs come from chickens.

*These White Leghorn chickens live on a farm.*

A female chicken is called a hen.

This chicken is a White Leghorn **hen**. You will learn how a chicken is born, grows up, has babies, gets old, and dies. This is the chicken's life cycle.

How does the hen's life cycle start?

# Laying Eggs

The **hen** starts life as an egg. The mother hen lays her eggs in a nest. There is a baby chicken in each egg. A baby chicken is called a **chick**.

*The eggs are white and oval-shaped with hard shells.*

The mother hen lays one egg a day. When she has laid about five eggs, she sits on them.

Chicks growing in the eggs need to keep warm.

When does the chick **hatch**?

7

# Hatching

Three weeks later, the mother **hen** hears a tapping sound. The eggs are starting to **hatch**.

*Chicks are pecking through the eggshells*

8

The **chick** uses her hard **beak** to crack the **eggshell**. Then, she pushes her body out of her egg. Hatching is hard work!

What does the baby chick look like?

# A New Chick

The new **chick** has yellow feathers. Her feathers are wet. They quickly dry out. The feathers keep the chick warm.

A new chick has damp feathers.

*The feathers are soon dry and fluffy.*

Soon all the other chicks in the nest have **hatched**. They start **peeping** and looking around.

Does the chick stay close to her mother?

# Off Exploring

The **chick** is just one week old.
The chick stays close to her mother.
She follows her mother wherever
she goes.

*Chicks feel safe if they stay close to their mother.*

12

When she is older, the chick starts to explore the farmyard.

*The young chicks have special food. It looks like bread crumbs.*

13

# New Feathers

As the **chicks** grow, they change color. They have grown white feathers instead of their fluffy yellow ones.

*The chick has grown and has new feathers.*

By about six weeks old, the chick is much bigger. She starts to look more like her mother.

When does the chick leave her mother?

# Leaving Mother

The **chick** is now two months old. She is ready to leave her mother. The chick can now take care of herself.

The chicks are big enough to explore by themselves.

*The chicks nest in a wooden henhouse at night.*

On the farm, she lives with the other chicks. They live in a **pen** in the farmyard. There is space to run around.

What does the chick eat?

# Hungry Chicks

The older **chicks** get special chick food to eat. The food helps the chicks to grow and stay healthy.

*The food has grains, fat, and* **vitamins** *in it.*

The chicks peck in the ground for juicy worms and insects to eat. Sometimes the farmer gives the chicks bits of fruit.

When does the chick lay her first egg?

# First Egg

The **chick** is five months old and almost fully grown. She is now called a **hen**.

*One day, she sits in a quiet place and lays her first egg.*

The hen has not **mated**, so there are no chicks in her eggs. The farmer collects the eggs. These are the eggs we can buy in the store and eat.

What is a male chicken called?

# Cock-a-Doodle-Doo!

A male chicken is called a **rooster**. This rooster is about eight months old.

*A rooster looks and sounds different from a hen.*

The rooster looks after the **hens.** He chases away other roosters. If a hen wanders off, he runs after her.

# Time to Mate

The **hen** is one year old. She is ready to **mate**. The **rooster** mates with the hen.

After she mates, the hen can lay eggs with **chicks** in them. The chicks **hatch** after 21 days.

# Staying Safe

Sometimes a hungry fox sneaks into the farmyard. Foxes steal **hens** to eat from the henhouse.

If she stays safe, a hen can live until
she is about seven years old.
A **rooster** can live until he is about
ten years old.

# Life Cycle of a Chicken

**1**
Mother **hen**
lays eggs
(day 1)

**2**
**Chick hatches**
(21 days)

**6**
Hen and
**rooster mate**
(1 year old)

**3**
Chick stays with
its mother
(1 week old)

**5**
Chick leaves
its mother
(2 months old)

**4**
Chick grows
white feathers
(6–7 weeks old)

# Chicken Map

tail

feathers

eyes

beak

feet

wings

# Glossary

**beak**  hard covering over a bird's mouth

**chick**  baby chicken

**eggshell**  hard covering around an egg

**hatch**  when an egg breaks open and a chick comes out

**hen**  female chicken

**mate**  when a male and female come together to make young

**peeping**  sound a chick makes

**pen**  part of the farmyard where chickens live

**rooster**  male chicken

**vitamins**  goodness in food that keeps animals healthy

# More Books to Read

Bell, Rachael. *Farm Animals: Chickens*. Chicago: Heinemann Library, 2000.

Ganeri, Anita. *Nature's Patterns: Animal Life Cycles*. Chicago: Heinemann Library, 2005.

Parker, Victoria. *Life as a Chicken*. Chicago: Raintree, 2004.

Royston, Angela. *Life as a Chicken*. Chicago: Heinemann Library, 1998.

Saunders-Smith, Gail. *Chickens*. Mankato, Minn.: Pebble, 1997.

Schwartz, David M. *Life Cycles: Chicken*. Milwaukee: Gareth Stevens, 2001.

# Index